SOURDOUGH

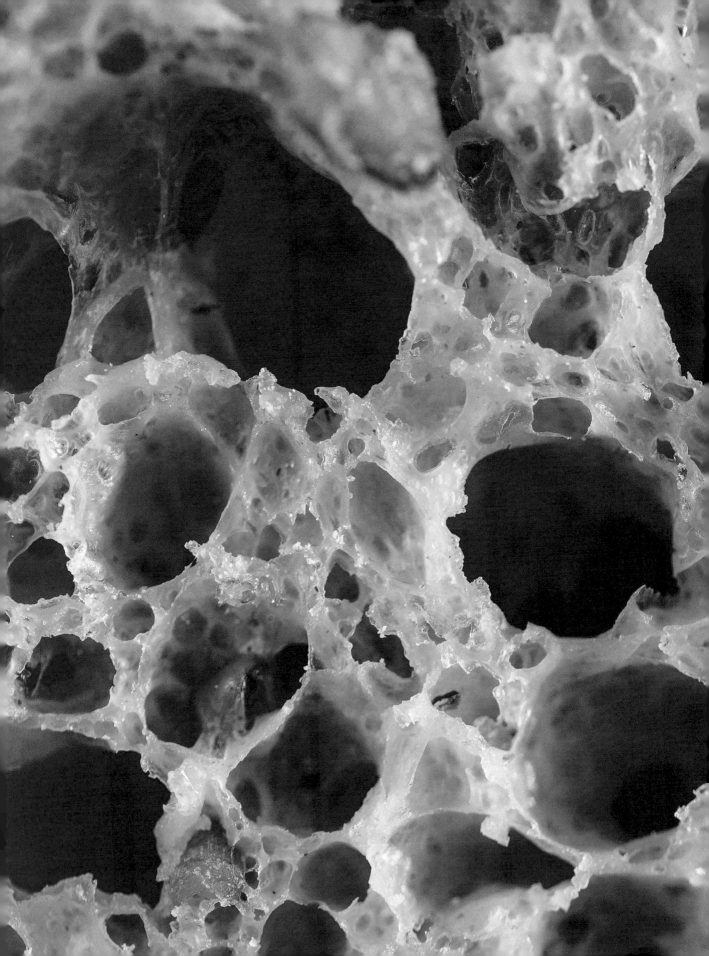

JOIN THE SOURDOUGH REVOLUTION ON INSTAGRAM @ILLEBROD

CASPER ANDRÉ LUGG & MARTIN IVAR HVEEM FJELD
are two young home bakers, from Fredrikstad, Norway. Over the last five
years they have developed their passion for sourdough baking and have shared their
enthusiasm with a growing number of followers through their Instagram account
@illebrod. They are committed to using time-honoured techniques coupled
with ancient grains and flour. Casper works as a full time writer and
Martin runs a small sourdough bakery in Oslo, Norway.

SOURDOUGH

CASPER ANDRÉ LUGG & MARTIN IVAR HVEEM FJELD

modern books

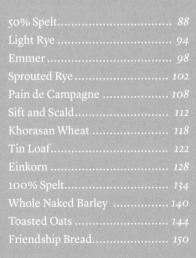

AMAZING FLAVOUR

FOREWORD BY VANESSA KIMBELL

Bread is older than metal. Archeological evidence traces it back past BC 10,000 and there is magic in making it yourself. Sourdough is a symbiotic relationship of wild yeast and lactic acid bacteria to ferment your bread. It is the oldest form of baking. For the past 120 years bread has become a fast dough production commodity, and it is fair to say that we lost our way as production became industrialized, but now there is a movement to reclaim good bread. This is not just a revival, nor just a moment of culinary fashion; sourdough has never been more relevant or exciting.

Long slow fermentation creates bread with amazing flavour and texture, and it gives you a loaf that has extraordinary health properties. Clinical studies have shown that long slow fermented bread made with sourdough lowers the GI of the bread, so your body will assimilate it more slowly, which can help regulate blood sugar. There is also an increasing body of evidence that long fermentation helps to break down the wheat into a food that is more easily digestible, so many of the anecdotal reports of people being able to digest sourdough more easily are being corroborated by science.

One of the things that seems to concern people most when they start to bake sourdough is that it is a time consuming or complicated process. It's actually quite the opposite. It is simply flour, salt and water with a live culture, left to ferment, stretched and folded, shaped and baked. If I am taking it really slowly, the sum total of time to bake a loaf is perhaps 15 – 20 minutes, over 36 hours. It is simply a matter of familiarizing yourself with a process, which is well worth mastering. The lactic acid also means that it lasts longer than commercial breads, the acids hold off the staling process. As a rough guide a loaf may last as long as the time it is left to ferment.

I particularly like the wholesome approach of this book, which will not just teach you to make sourdough bread, but also get you out of the kitchen to meet the millers in your area. Sourdough is far far more than just about the bread. It is about connecting people and process. Whilst the sourdough is a collective of microorganisms that co-exist in a pot, it seems to extend its principles of the symbiotic relationship beyond, to the world around us and suddenly your sourdough becomes part of life.

VANESSA KIMBELL teaches at the Sourdough School in Northamptonshire and is a regular contributor to BBC Radio 4's *Food Programme*.

BAKER'S NOTES

Baking your own delicious home-made bread is certainly achievable – all it takes is patience and practice. The following points, however, are also useful to know.

AUTOLYSIS: Autolysis (also known as 'autolyse' or the 'delayed-salt' method) takes a lot of the effort out of making sourdough and will help you achieve the bread's remarkable texture. The term is Greek for 'self-digestion', but in the context of sourdough baking it can be translated as allowing the dough to do the hard work.

By mixing your ingredients together carefully and leaving the dough alone for one hour, a solid gluten structure forms just like the one created during normal kneading. Autolysis also contributes to creating a stretchy dough that is comfortable to handle, and which will form large air pockets and retain the aromatic gases produced during fermentation. The salt is added only after autolysis, which ensures that the dough develops better elasticity and strength. See the Basic Bread recipe (page 50) for how the method is employed.

BAKING PERCENTAGES: In each list of ingredients, you will find a baking percentage in parentheses. We have found that baking percentages are very useful in demonstrating how much there is of an ingredient in relation to the total amount of flour, regardless of how many loaves you are baking. In our recipes, the amount of flour is always 500 g. If the water quantity is 400 g, it will be at 80%, 100 g leaven is 20% and so on. So if you double, or even triple the recipe, the percentages remain the same.

FLOURS: Throughout we refer to strong white bread flour and by this we mean the best quality, organic and unbleached wheat flour you can afford (see pages 156–7 for a list of ingredient suppliers). The locally grown, stonemilled flour we are used to in Norway is generally a bit weaker than bread flour. This can give a more tender, custardy crumb. So if you happen to find a medium strong, stone milled, white bread flour (11 g protein) you might want to try that instead.

MIXING: We always recommend hand mixing since a machine will mix more intensively and you won't gain the experience of knowing when your dough has the right feel and texture.

WATER: The quantity of water you use in the dough is always relative, because different flours have different levels of absorbency. A bag of flour that has been on a store shelf for a few months has dried out more than fresh flour and will therefore be 'thirstier' when you mix it with water.

If you find the dough is dry, you can add more water when mixing in the salt, but go slowly and add no more than 25 g of water at a time. This water must be as warm as the amount you first added to the dough, or even a few degrees warmer. See our trouble-shooting tips on page 81 if your dough feels too wet and is hard to work with.

1

FLOUR, WATER
& SALT

FLOUR, WATER & SALT

Sourdough is the original baked bread. The methods and recipes in this book build upon a practice that is more than 5,000 years old. The basic elements have always been the same: mix flour and water, then allow the dough to ferment and rise by itself.

Anyone can bake good sourdough bread. You just have to give it time and attention and use the best ingredients possible. One always gets more out of using raw materials from dedicated organic farmers and millers who care for the soil and the processing of grain.

Flour, water and salt – that is all you need. Our method does not require much physical work as it is first and foremost about allowing natural processes to take place at their own pace. It is a flexible way of baking to which most schedules can be adapted. Time, however, is critical. In fact, time can almost be viewed as the fourth ingredient. It is time that allows the flavours of the grain to mature, which gives bread its unique quality.

There are many different grains available and some are thousands of years old. In our native Scandinavia they were mostly overrun by the emergence of modern agriculture. But thanks to some enthusiasts, ancient grains – such as einkorn, emmer, spelt, naked barley and rye meal – are being cultivated again.

The roots of organic grain husks run deep into the earth and extract all the nutrients they need right from the soil. Neither spraying nor artificial fertiliser are necessary. The result is extra flavour and nutrition. All the breads in this book are baked with organic grain and stoneground flour from small independent farms and mills, not far from where we live. When flour is ground on stone and not in industrial roller mills, the grain is exposed to minimal heat, which helps preserve its nutrients and flavour. This gentler treatment preserves the oil from the germ, providing plenty of aromas from the grain to pass on to the bread.

Baking with sourdough may seem complicated at first. Once you have had the dough in your hands a few times, however, you will find that the learning curve is steep but rewarding. There's only one way to become a good sourdough baker, and that is by baking as much as possible.

There are many paths to good sourdough bread, but the method we present in this book produces, in our opinion, the best results. It is a method that perfectly suits baking with stoneground flour from small-scale production, which often have weaker baking properties than commercial flour. When these loaves are successful, they result in an airy and moist crumb, a caramelised and crisp crust and have a distinctive flavour from the grain. Good luck!

2

SOURDOUGH STARTER

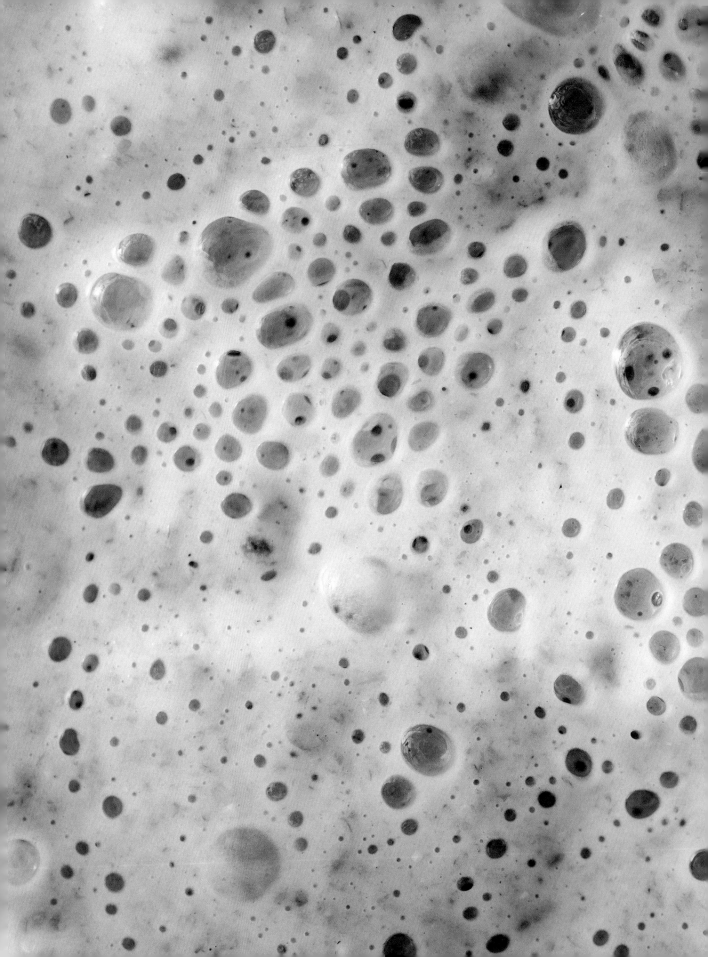

MAKING A STARTER

B aking sourdough bread requires a 'sourdough starter'. This is a mixture of flour and water that has been left long enough at room temperature so that it has begun to ferment and become a seething culture of yeast spores and lactic acid bacteria. The yeast and bacteria are found naturally in the grain shell parts, in the air, on our hands – in short, everywhere. In the flour mixture, they feed and multiply as soon as they come into contact with water. It is this process that enables sourdough baking. The yeast spores produce air (CO_2), which makes the dough rise, and the bacteria produce acid. This in turn helps to strengthen the dough's gluten network and it also brings some tremendous aromas to your freshly baked breads.

A sourdough starter (hereafter we'll simply call it a 'starter') can live a long life if you just take care of it. When we make a starter from scratch, we simply mix fresh flour and water, and then let it sit in a warm place. After a while, the mixture will begin to ferment by itself. At first, the fermentation process goes slowly. But as you follow the steps in the following pages, the micro-organisms will multiply, eventually forming a natural balance between yeast spores and lactic acid bacteria in your new starter. In just one week, your glass will be full of life and you'll be ready to get started on your first baking session.

YOU WILL NEED

Fine wholegrain rye flour, stoneground and organic. Organic strong white bread flour.

Two 1-litre glass jars with lids.

Water at 27–30°C (mix cold water with boiled water).

Digital kitchen scale.

DAY 1, MORNING

Mix 50 g finely ground wholegrain rye flour with 80 g water at 30°C in one of the glass jars. The mixture should be quite moist. Place the lid on loosely so it is not completely airtight and let it sit for 24 hours in a warm place, preferably around 25°C, until the next morning.

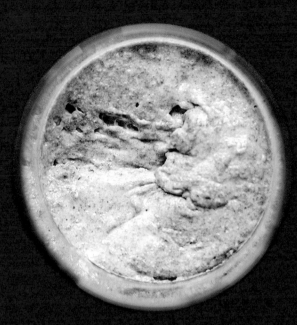

DAY 2, MORNING

Do you notice a distinctive smell? That mild, sour aroma is fermentation. If you stir the mixture a little, you might also see that it has become slightly porous and bulging. If so, the process has started. If it smells a little stale, like wet grass, leave it to sit for one more day.

Mix in 50 g fine wholegrain rye flour and 80 g water at 30°C. Let sit for 24 hours.

DAY 3, MORNING

You will find that the mixture has grown (probably to about double the volume of the original) and that some bubbles have formed on the surface and at the sides. The smell will be reminiscent of wheat beer, biscuits and crackers, with a hint of acidity.

Mix in 50 g fine wholegrain rye flour and 80 g water at 30°C. Let sit for 24 hours.

DAY 4, MORNING

Now, when you smell and look at the mixture, there should be no doubt that there is a fermentation culture brewing with life. The mixture now contains so many active micro-organisms that you can use a small portion to ferment a larger batch of flour and water.

Add 50 g of your sourdough culture to the second glass. Feed it with 50 g fine wholegrain rye flour and 80 g water at 30°C. Let sit for 24 hours.

DAY 5, MORNING

You should now clearly see that air bubbles have formed inside the glass, and the mixture has greatly increased in volume. At this point you're ready to begin the regular feeding of your starter.

Put 30 g starter in a new clean glass. Feed it with 50 g fine wholegrain rye flour, 50 g strong white bread flour and 130 g water at 30°C. Let sit for 12 hours. You could now bake with this, but to be on the safe side, we recommend that you feed it twice more before setting your first leaven (see Setting the Leaven, page 32), or putting it in the refrigerator if you will not be baking immediately.

FEEDING THE STARTER

T he micro-organisms in the starter eat the sugar released from the flour by starch enzymes. When this 'food' has been consumed, the yeast and bacteria need new food in the form of more flour and water. For the starter to stay in good shape, it should be fed at least once a week.

If you keep the starter in the refrigerator it is enough to feed it once or twice a week, but be sure to feed it twice before baking. The first feed should be approximately 24 hours prior to baking and the second around 12 hours prior. If you bake more than twice a week, it is best to keep the starter at room temperature. We recommend that you feed it twice a day, morning and night, every day. Otherwise you risk it becoming too acidic, thereby creating an imbalance between the yeast and bacteria, which will have a negative effect on both taste and expansion.

FEEDING THE STARTER:

1. Remove your starter from the refrigerator at night.

2. Pour 50 g starter into a new, clean glass. Add 130 g water at 30°C and 100 g flour mixture (50/50 fine wholegrain rye and strong white bread flour). Stir together well. The consistency should be similar to waffle batter. If it is thicker or thinner, adjust by using more or less water.

3. Allow the starter to sit in a warm place until the next morning, with the lid on loosely to allow air to get in. The starter should always rise to its apex, approximately triple the volume, which usually takes between 10–14 hours, before putting it back in the refrigerator, feeding it again or using it to set the leaven. If you are unsure whether or not it will grow more, wait until you see that it has begun to sag slightly.

If you are not planning to bake the same day, put the starter back in the refrigerator. If you will be baking later that day, feed the starter again and leave it on the work surface until the afternoon.

SETTING THE LEAVEN

E ach baking session begins with setting a leaven, which matures over a few hours. This is a blend of your starter and fresh flour and water. It is the leaven that makes the bread dough rise. This occurs when the sourdough culture eats sugars from the flour, broken down by starch enzymes. When the yeast eats the sugar, this produces CO_2, which makes the bread dough airy. The air is trapped within the pockets formed by the dough's gluten structure.

It is important that the leaven is allowed to progress properly before being used in bread dough. It needs to have swelled and become porous and some bubbles should have formed on the surface. You can also tell by the smell: there should be a scent of mild acidity, combined with a fruity and ripe sweetness. To be on the safe side the first few times that you bake, we recommend you do a floating test. Put a teaspoon of the leaven in a glass of water – if it floats, it means that the yeast has begun producing CO_2 and is ready to raise larger dough. If it does not float, allow it to mature for another hour or two. Without a proper leaven, the dough will not rise at the pace we need, nor will it develop good gluten strength – which

is where the acidity from the leaven plays a crucial role.

It is also important not to let the leaven sit for too long beyond the recommended time because it will affect the taste of the final loaf. If you allow the leaven to sit for too long, it will develop a sharp acidity that propagates in the dough and can overpower the mild flavours of the grain.

The length of time the leaven needs to mature before it is ready depends on how much starter you use in the mixture. The latter can vary depending on how much time you have.

It is wise to plan a little when baking your first sourdough bread. Make sure to set aside time to feed the starter and to set the leaven before starting to bake. If you want to bake tomorrow evening, you must feed the starter tonight, tomorrow morning and set the leaven tomorrow afternoon. If you want to bake late tomorrow morning, feed the starter early today, later tonight and set the leaven early tomorrow morning. If you want to start baking as soon as you wake up, set a leaven the night before with slightly less starter and let it sit overnight.

Here are the two versions we use (creating enough leaven for one loaf):

---

20 g mature starter / 40 g flour mixture (50/50 fine wholegrain rye and strong white bread flour) / 40 g water at 30°C. Let sit at room temperature for 4–8 hours.

40 g mature starter / 30 g flour mixture (50/50 fine wholegrain rye and strong white bread flour) / 30 g water at 30°C. Let sit at room temperature for 2–4 hours.

3

BASIC
BREAD
RECIPE

EQUIPMENT

Dough scraper

Cast iron pot
or firebricks

Sourdough starter

Razor blade or cutting knife

Timer

Digital kitchen scale

Bowl with warm water

Flour, to sprinkle

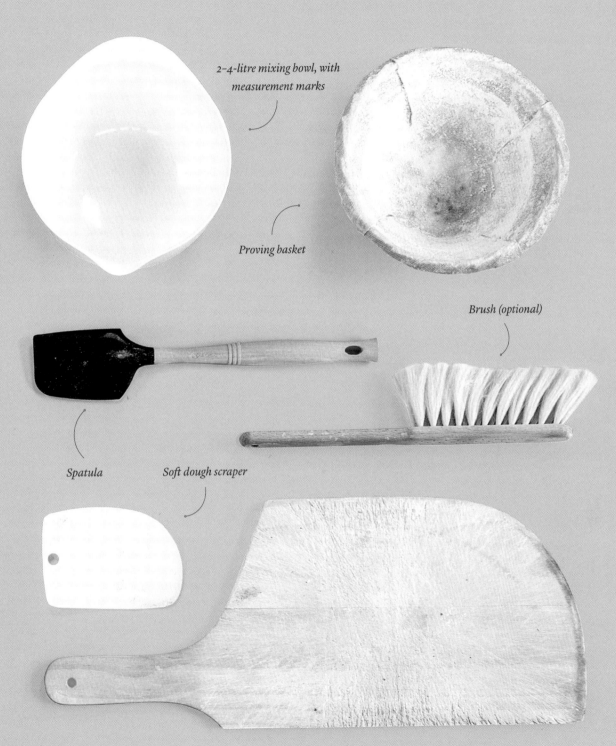

2-4-litre mixing bowl, with measurement marks

Proving basket

Brush (optional)

Spatula

Soft dough scraper

Bread peel, or similar

BASIC BREAD RECIPE

This recipe is our fundamental method and provides the basis for every recipe in the book. What changes from recipe to recipe is the list of ingredients – in particular, how much and what kind of wholegrain flour you have in the dough, the quantity of water and whether you have any added flavours. The Basic Bread recipe is a good place to start, because it produces dough that is easy to handle for the first few times you bake. The 30% wholegrain spelt gives the bread a distinct flavour of grain, while the relatively high proportion of strong white bread flour contributes to an expansive and airy baked product.

The dough should rise by a third in the mixing bowl over 3½ hours. This presupposes a certain temperature in the room and in the water you use. If it is cold in the room, the rising will be slower. If it is warmer, the rising will be faster. Neither will necessarily spoil the baking but it might be temporarily inconvenient. The ideal room temperature is between 24 and 26°C. If you find a way to keep it warm in a small, closed room or to heat up the kitchen, the results will be the same.

You will quickly notice the dough's consistency changing quite a bit during the baking process. When first mixed, it is tacky and sticks quickly to one's hands, and it may feel as if it does not stay together at all. But eventually it will come together, the gluten bonds will strengthen, the dough will feel smoother and it will stay together more. And it will not stick as easily to the bowl or to your hands. You will also notice the dough changing from being fairly lifeless and heavy to being more light and airy, with large bubbles appearing on the surface.

The water quantity given in the recipes should be understood as a guide. We tend to bake with as much hydration (water quantity in the dough) as the flour we use permits, because this results in moister bread. It is quite difficult, however, to handle very wet dough. Therefore, we recommend that you start with the lowest amount of water suggested in the recipe and then work up from there as you become more and more comfortable working with the dough.

If you want to bake more than one loaf at a time, just multiply the ingredient quantities by the desired number of loaves and later divide the dough with the dough scraper before the first shaping in step 5 of the method.

Bake with all your senses wide open! As with so many things, sourdough baking can be approached as a science, but ultimately it comes down to practice.

INGREDIENTS

FOR THE LEAVEN

40 g mature starter
30 g water at 30°C
15 g strong white bread flour
15 g fine wholegrain spelt flour

FOR THE BREAD DOUGH
Baking percentages in parentheses

150 g fine wholegrain spelt flour (30%)
350 g strong white bread flour (70%)
375–425 g water at 30°C (75–85%)
10 g finely ground unrefined sea salt (2%)
100 g leaven (20%)

STEP BY STEP

SET THE LEAVEN

You have fed your starter twice in the last day and it is now mature and full of life. Now you're ready to set the leaven. When you mix a leaven, you are doing the same thing as when feeding the starter with flour and water, only with slightly different measurements – and everything takes place in a mixing bowl.

OPTION 1
Setting the leaven for
2-4 hours:

Measure out 40 g mature starter, 30 g water, 15 g strong white bread flour and 15 g fine wholegrain spelt flour in a mixing bowl. Stir together well. Allow the leaven to mature for 2-4 hours.

OPTION 2
Setting the leaven for
4-8 hours:

Measure out 20 g mature starter, 40 g water, 20 g strong white bread flour and 20 g fine wholegrain spelt flour. Stir together well. Allow the leaven to mature for 4-8 hours. (In the other recipes, we include option 1 only).

Return the starter to the refrigerator.

2

MIX FLOUR, WATER AND LEAVEN
(AUTOLYSIS - SEE PAGE 12)

The water for the dough should be about 28-30°C. Pour 375-425 g water into the bowl with the leaven. Loosen up the mixture in the water with your fingers. Add the flour. Use your hands to stir, making sure everything is well mixed together. Gather the dough by scraping down any excess from the edges with a spatula or soft dough scraper. Loosely cover the bowl and let it sit for an hour.

PINCH IN THE SALT

Measure out the required amount of salt and sprinkle it over the dough. Use your thumb and forefinger to pinch the dough to squeeze out small 'balls' in the bowl. Do this a few times until you feel the dough begin to tighten and it becomes harder to pinch. We do this to break up the dough's gluten network, allowing it to reorganise itself, multiply and form stronger bonds. Gather the dough by scraping down the excess from the edges. Let it rest for 30 minutes.

AUTOLYSIS (SEE PAGE 12)

PINCH IN THE SALT

STRETCH AND FOLD

First dip your hand in a bowl of warm water, then push your fingers between the dough and the side of the bowl and grab the underside of the dough. Stretch it slightly and fold it over towards the opposite side of the bowl. Repeat this process, working your way around the bowl, 5 to 8 times, until you feel the dough has firmed up properly. The goal here is to stretch the gluten network, not to break it (as you did in the 'pinching' process in step 3). Cover and leave to rest for 30 minutes.

Repeat the stretching and folding twice at 30-minute intervals. After the last folding, allow the dough to rest until it has increased in volume by about a third. This can take anywhere from 30–90 minutes, but will usually take about an hour.

Use a mixing bowl with measurement marks, so you can track the dough rising with more precision. With the quantities we give in the recipes, the dough has increased in volume by a third when it reaches approximately the 1-litre mark.

5

THE FIRST SHAPING

Scrape the dough onto a well-floured surface. Have a bowl of flour nearby so you can dip your hand in flour if the dough becomes too sticky. Use the dough scraper to fold the dough over itself a few times from different sides, and then all the way around so that it folds face down on the table. Use the dough scraper to firm up the dough, by pushing it from different angles. The dough should stick slightly to the table while you do this, so that it becomes taught and has thick edges. If the dough scraper sticks to the dough, sprinkle some flour on it before continuing.

BENCH REST

Sprinkle a little flour over the dough and let it rest for 15–25 minutes, or until the dough has become a little flatter around the edges. The aim here is for the dough's gluten bonds to relax, which will make the next shaping easier.

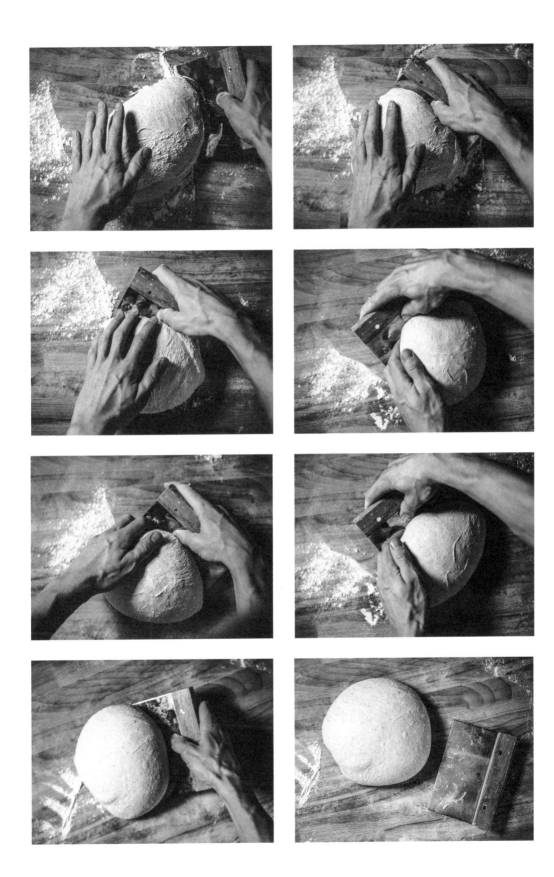

7

FINAL SHAPING

Flour your proving basket well; use a little more than you might think necessary the first few times just to be on the safe side, as it is very frustrating when the dough sticks to the basket! Eventually you will figure out just how much flour you need – ideally the finished bread should have a nice contrast between white flour and a dark, golden crust. We use a 50/50 mixture of strong white bread flour and rice flour to flour the basket. Rice flour has harder particles that won't swell upon contact with the wet dough, thereby making the dough release itself more easily from the basket. If you do not have rice flour, we recommend using fine wholegrain rye flour.

Flour the dough and work surface next to it (as above, it is better to use too much than too little flour in the beginning). Use the dough scraper to loosen the dough from the surface and to flip it over so that the floured part is face down on the floured surface. Grasp the top of the dough and fold it in towards the centre. Grasp the left side of the dough and fold it in towards the centre, then the same with the right side and finally the underneath. Now you have a square. Grab one corner, stretch it slightly and fold it in towards the centre. When all four corners are folded in, grasp the topside and flip the dough over so the seam is down against the surface and the smooth side is facing up. If the dough still feels loose, tighten it up a little with the dough scraper, as you did in the first shaping, before lifting it over in the proving basket so that it will lie with the folds uppermost.

The step-by-step photographs on the following pages demonstrate how to go about the final shaping process.

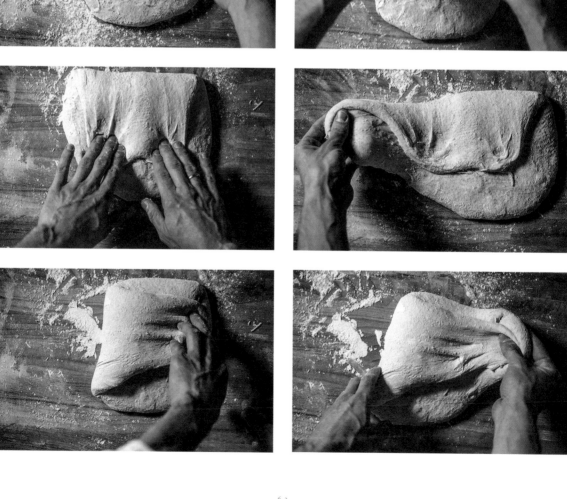

BASKET PROVING

The length of the basket proving will vary according to how much the dough has risen in the bowl. If it rose by more than a third, you may want to start with only an hour in the basket, but 1½–2 hours is usually just right. This is where you will need to just gain experience. If you allow the dough to rise even a bit too much in the proving basket the first time, you will see that 'craters' form when the bread is in the oven and it becomes flat. If this happens, you can reduce the rising time in the basket the next time. But be daring! Perfectly fermented dough provides both volume and an open and light crumb. After rising in the basket, place the dough in the refrigerator for cold proving (see the next step).

If you miss out on the dough's rising in the basket altogether, you can do this step after the cold rising while the oven is heating up. Baking room-temperature dough produces bread with slightly different characteristics – the crust might be slightly less caramelised but the crumb can be more airy. You just have to experiment. When baking in a cast iron pot or casserole, the dough should not be room temperature when it's placed in the pot, as it can be difficult to get a warm dough into the pot undamaged.

COLD PROVING

Put the dough in the refrigerator. You do not have to cover it unless the dough is very dry. If you want to bake in the evening, the cold rising needs to occur overnight; if you want to bake in the early to late morning, the cold rising needs to occur in the afternoon and evening the day before. While you're sleeping or busy with other things, the dough can continue to develop even more flavour without rising too much. This step is also known as 'retarding' because the cold slows fermentation. Cold rising produces lots of extra flavour in the bread and the crust becomes even more caramelised than if you continued rising at room temperature. Moreover, this process increases the nutrients that are good for the body. As long as your refrigerator effectively slows the rising process, you can let the dough rest there for up to 36 hours, but the optimum is 12–24 hours. Do what best suits your schedule.

BAKING

The two most important elements of bread baking are a strong, absorbent heat and moisture (steam). Both are possible to achieve in a conventional oven, either using a preheated cast iron pot with a tight lid, or by baking on scorching hot firebricks. The latter requires a little more effort, but it also produces, in our opinion, a better crust and a more rustic bread, which is allowed to expand more freely.

We can divide the baking process into two parts. In the first part, the dough should expand in a moist environment. The moisture from the steam ensures that the dough does not solidify and stick together and it will allow the scoring made on top to burst open while the dough expands to its full potential. In the final stage of baking, the bread crust is formed – this is where it is an advantage to get most of the steam out of the oven, so that the crust becomes crisp and deeply caramelised.

If you're baking in a cast iron pot or casserole with a lid, the dough creates its own damp environment, since the water that evaporates from the dough becomes trapped in the pot. If you're baking on firebricks, the steam must be added in the form of boiled water poured into a bowl on the lowest level in the oven. Most modern stoves are designed to wick away moisture during cooking, which is the opposite of what we want in the first few minutes. One way to make the oven more airtight is to tape up the air vents next to the burners.

BAKING IN A CAST IRON POT
4½-6½ litres, 24-28 cm in diameter

Place your clean cast iron pot, including the lid and metal knob, on the bottom shelf of the oven and turn the heat on to the highest temperature the oven can reach. Allow the oven and pot to warm up for 60 minutes, setting the timer. When the time has elapsed, remove the dough from the refrigerator; leave it on the counter. Use oven gloves to remove the pot from the oven and remove the lid. Sprinkle a thin layer of flour on the underside of the dough (the one facing upwards in the basket) and flip the dough from the proving basket onto a lightly floured bread peel or the like. It is now time to score the dough.

SCORING: Scoring dough gives bread soul and the feel of being baked by hand. The primary purpose is to give the dough weak points where the surface can 'burst' and the bread can expand. We vary between a few fairly simple patterns that we choose according to the dough we are working with (coarse, light, strong, weak).

To begin with, we recommend a simple square because scoring can be a bit tricky the first few times. But feel free to experiment later. Here are a few things to pay close attention to when scoring:

- Do not take the dough out of the proofing basket until you are ready with the scoring blade – it should be the last thing you do before the dough goes in the oven.
- Keep the blade at an angle when you score. This forms a protective 'lip' that allows the cut to retain moisture and to crack more smoothly.
- Be quick and firm when scoring. Pulling the blade slowly through the dough will produce an uneven and deep incision.
- Score approximately 5 mm deep. If the dough is slightly under-fermented, your incision can go a little deeper. If it is a little over-fermented, the incision should be quite shallow.

Once you've scored the dough, slide it from the bread peel into the pot. This also requires some practice – don't worry if the dough goes in slightly skewed the first few times, as you will soon learn the technique. And the pot will shape the dough in such a way that you almost always end up with presentable bread.

Cover with the lid and place the pot in the oven (using oven gloves). Turn down the heat to 240°C and bake for 20 minutes. When the timer goes off, remove the lid and continue to bake, uncovered, at 230°C for 20 minutes more, or until the bread has a deep golden crust.

BAKING ON FIREBRICKS

Buy six firebricks at your local building supplier. The length and width are standard dimensions, but the thickness will vary. Look for the thinnest, approximately 2 cm thick. Six of these will fit perfectly in any generic household oven. Set the bricks on a rack on the secondlowest shelf. Place a roasting tin on the bottom shelf under the firebricks.

You can also use a pizza baking stone, but these are usually quite thin and do not generate as much heat. The base will therefore be softer as the bread cools, but during baking, it will expand and develop normally.

Preheat the oven to its highest temperature for 1½–2 hours. Boil 400 ml water and put it into something from which it is easy to pour. Remove the dough from the refrigerator, sprinkle a thin layer of flour over the bottom of the dough (the one facing upwards in the basket) and flip the dough from the basket onto a lightly floured bread peel. Score with the desired pattern and slide the dough onto the bricks. Pour the boiling hot water into the roasting tin and close the oven door. Bake at 240°C for 20 minutes, then open the oven door to release the steam. You can also rotate the bread a bit for more uniform baking. Continue baking for another 20 to 25 minutes at 230°C. The bread is done when it has a deep golden colour on both the top and bottom – we like it dark!

If you find it difficult to keep the dough intact when moving it onto the bricks, you can tilt it out of the basket onto parchment paper, then slide it onto the scorching hot bricks. The paper can be removed after 15 to 20 minutes, so that the bread will be in direct contact with the bricks during the final stage of baking.

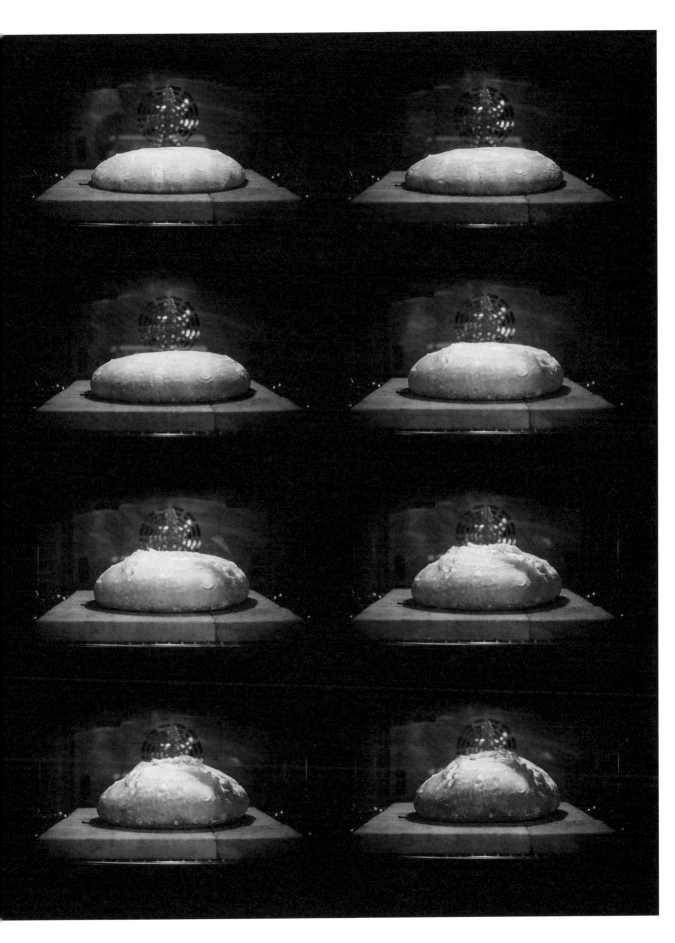

TROUBLE-
SHOOTING

WHAT WENT WRONG?

Baking with sourdough is never an entirely predictable process. The living organisms we are working with are directly affected by factors such as how we take care of them, changing temperatures and humidity, what kind of flour we use, plus a number of other factors that are difficult to anticipate as they occur on a microscopic level. There are still some key points that you can keep track of, and if you are aware of these you will get much better results.

THE DOUGH CRACKS WHILE RESTING ON THE WORK SURFACE

This can happen if you use very weak flour. We use locally grown flour from small farms and the gluten strength of these naturally varies according to how the season's weather has been. The solution may be to scale down the amount of water in the dough (70% is generally safe). You can also scale down the percentage of wholegrain flour in the dough.

THE DOUGH BECOMES STUCK IN THE PROVING BASKET

This can happen if you are baking with wet dough and do not have enough flour in the basket. It is imperative to use the correct mixture to flour the basket. We use a mixture of rice flour and sifted flour because rice flour does not swell as quickly when in contact with water and stays dry longer. This allows the dough to release more easily from the basket.

THE BREAD RISES MORE SLOWLY THAN THE TIME GIVEN IN THE RECIPE

The first thing to look at when fermentation does not go as planned is the starter. If this is not right, it will affect the entire process. The best way to ensure that the starter is fully active is to feed it often, preferably morning and evening. Many bakers keep the starter in the refrigerator between baking sessions. But if you're unsure whether it is active enough, we recommend that you feed it morning and evening over two days and watch how it evolves. It should have reached its peak in the course of 6 hours, but this depends upon the temperature in your kitchen.

The best rising temperature is above room temperature, usually around 24–26°C. So if your dough rises slowly, the solution may be to warm up the room a bit more when you are baking. Also, remember to use warm water at about 30°C when feeding the starter, setting the leaven and mixing the dough.

If the dough rises slowly and the bread becomes compact and stale in flavour, the explanation may be that your leaven was not properly set. Make sure the next time that the leaven is set before using it in the bread dough.

THE DOUGH FEELS VERY WET AND IS IMPOSSIBLE TO HANDLE ON THE WORK SURFACE

This occurs if you have used too much water in the dough. There is no rule for water quantity because all flours have different absorbency. The solution is to start low (70%) and then add a little more water after autolysis, when you add the salt. Be careful not to increase the water quantity by more than 25 g (5%) at a time, making sure also that this water is not colder than the water you used when you first mixed the dough - it can even be a few degrees warmer. Handling wet dough requires a lot of skill and technique. As you get used to it and feel comfortable with the shaping method, you can increase the amount of water. You may also find that the dough feels wet and flattens out too much on the work surface because the fermentation is slow. The dough is not really wetter - it is just weaker and has less elasticity because the leaven has not developed acid in the dough fast enough. Acid strengthens gluten bonds and strong dough can carry more water.

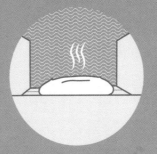

THE DOUGH GOES FLAT WHILE BAKING

The dough can go flat while baking if you have allowed the fermentation process to go on too long; this is called 'over-fermentation'. The dough will not have any strength left to expand in the heat because the fermentation process broke down the strong gluten bonds. The solution is to shorten the proving basket fermentation time. Make sure also that it is cool enough in your refrigerator. If the problem persists, try to use a little less leaven, for example, 75 g (15%) instead of 100 g (20%). You can use this combination: 15 g starter, 15 g sifted flour, 15 g wholegrain flour and 30 g water at 30°C. Allow to mature over 3-6 hours.

THE BREAD COMES OFF THE BAKING PLATE AND DOES NOT EXPAND UPWARD

Just because the bread does not expand a lot upward does not mean something is wrong. The more water you use in the dough, the less it will expand upward as it will spread out more, but the crumb will be more moist. If the dough rises from underneath, however, and the scoring does not spring open, this is usually a sign that you have used too much water in the dough, or the fermentation process has been too slow. It may also be due to the oven being too hot - perhaps you forgot to turn down the heat to 240°C before baking. Properly fermented dough will sag outward within the first minute of baking before the dough begins to expand, mostly in the centre but also around the edges. You may also find that the dough does not just rise from below, but instead cracks on the sides. This is often a sign that the dough is under-fermented, or that the cooking environment in the oven is not ideal. Perhaps you have forgotten the water at the base of the oven to create steam during baking? In this case, the dough will mesh together on the surface from the direct radiant heat and then burst where it is weakest, always closest to the bottom. Use firebricks and be sure to preheat the oven well. Close off the air vent inside the oven with a little foil or tape the vent on the outside next to the burners.

RECIPES

50% SPELT

T his is the bread we bake most often. The large proportion of stoneground wholegrain spelt flour produces a substantial and nutritious bread with a mild, nutty flavour. This is also where we have challenged ourselves the most to get a soft, moist crumb despite the fact that this is a loaf with a high percentage of whole grain flour. This bread has, simply, shaped our method of baking.

Many of the spelt flours on the market are variations that have been crossed so many times with modern wheat that the flour has lost many of its original characteristics.

If you buy stoneground spelt from a smaller producer you will be on safer ground.

Spelt has predominantly good baking properties, but it does have softer gluten than ordinary wheat, which contributes to a fragile and light crumb that almost melts on the tongue. Stoneground spelt produces a velvety and supple dough, which is wonderful to work with. A good stoneground flour should feel oily when you rub it between your fingers – this means that the oils from the germ of the grain have been preserved, as well as much of its aroma.

INGREDIENTS
Baking percentage in parentheses

For the leaven:	*For the bread dough:*
40 g mature starter	*250 g fine wholegrain spelt flour (50%)*
30 g water at 30°C	*250 g strong white bread flour (50%)*
15 g strong white bread flour	*400–450 g water at 30°C (80–90%)*
15 g fine wholegrain spelt flour	*10 g finely ground unrefined sea salt (2%)*
	100 g leaven (20%)

1

SET THE LEAVEN

Measure out 40 g starter (which has been at room temperature for 6–24 hours since the last feeding), 30 g water, 15 g strong white bread flour and 15 g fine wholegrain spelt flour. Mix well, cover the bowl and allow the newly mixed leaven to mature for 2–4 hours. Put the starter back in the refrigerator.

2

MIX FLOUR, WATER AND LEAVEN (AUTOLYSIS)

Pour 400–450 g water into the bowl with the leaven. Dissolve the leaven in the water with your fingers. Add the specified amount of flour. Use your hands to make sure everything is well mixed together. Gather the dough by scraping down the excess from the edges with a spatula. Cover the bowl and let it sit for an hour (set the timer). Then follow the Basic Bread recipe from step 3 (see page 50).

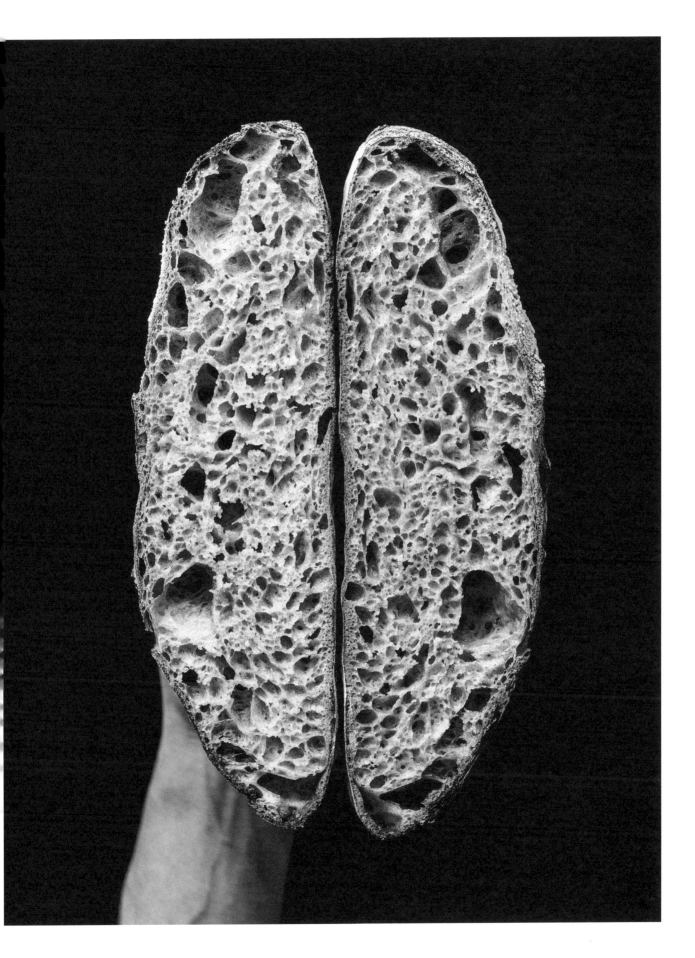

LIGHT RYE

Rye contains more sugar than other grains, which makes this bread extra sweet with a slightly thicker and more flavourful crust. Rye has a complex aroma, both sweet and earthy, and as with all other small-scale cultivation the grain's taste and properties are influenced by the climate and environment during the growth period, not to mention the way in which it is processed into flour. Rye can be difficult to bake with in high percentages, so for this recipe we chose to add 20% wholegrain, making it a darker country loaf. This amount of rye is sufficient for the characteristics of the grain to come through.

Dough with rye is sticky, so use a little more flour on the work surface than usual to shape the dough. It is also sensible to increase the amount of water because rye absorbs more water than other flours.

INGREDIENTS
Baking percentage in parentheses

For the leaven:
40 g mature starter
30 g water at 30°C
15 g strong white bread flour
15 g fine wholegrain rye flour

For the bread dough:
100 g fine wholegrain rye flour (20%)
400 g strong white bread flour (80%)
400–450 g water at 30°C (80–90%)
10 g finely ground unrefined sea salt (2%)
100 g leaven (20%)

1

SET THE LEAVEN

Measure out 40 g starter (which has been at room temperature for 6-24 hours since the last feeding), 30 g water, 15 g strong white bread flour and 15 g fine wholegrain rye flour. Mix well, cover the bowl and let the leaven mature for 2-4 hours.
Put the starter back in the refrigerator.

2

MIX FLOUR, WATER AND LEAVEN (AUTOLYSIS)

Pour 400-450 g water into the bowl with the leaven. Dissolve the leaven in the water with your fingers. Add the specified amount of flour. Use your hands to make sure everything is well mixed together. Gather the dough by scraping down the excess from the edges with a spatula. Cover the bowl and let it sit for an hour (set the timer).
Then follow the Basic Bread recipe from step 3 (see page 50).

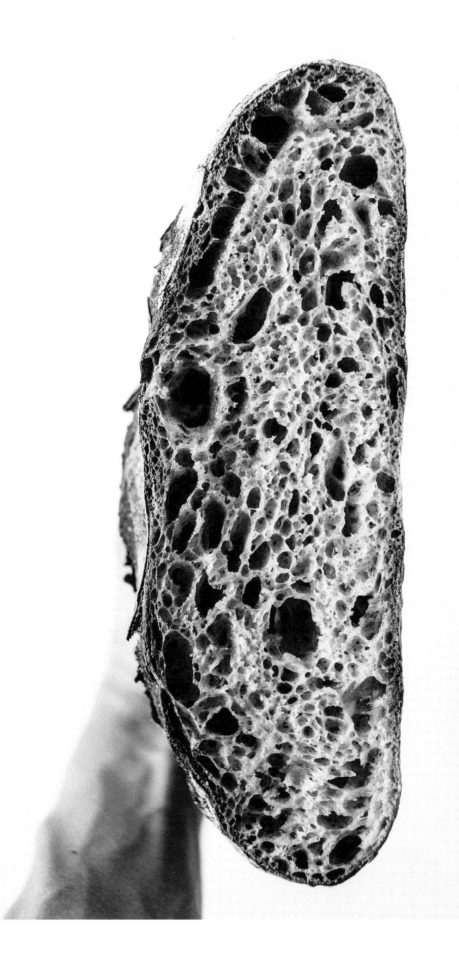

EMMER

W ith 40% fine wholegrain emmer, this is a bread with a lot of 'body' in its flavour, with touches of grass and hay. The bread has an almost reddish crust. Emmer is a member of the wheat family, like einkorn and spelt. We have tested this grain from small local mills and have experienced how things can vary by season, but the taste is always distinctive. The dough is great to handle, but its baking properties are generally slightly weaker than spelt and ordinary wheat and therefore the bread is prone to slightly less expansion. If the proper amount of time is spent fermenting, however, you can still achieve a delicate and open crumb with an outstanding dark aroma.

INGREDIENTS
Baking percentage in parentheses

For the leaven:	For the bread dough:
40 g mature starter	*200 g fine wholegrain emmer flour (40%)*
30 g water at 30°C	*300 g strong white bread flour (60%)*
15 g strong white bread flour	*375–425 g water at 30°C (75–85%)*
15 g fine wholegrain emmer flour	*10 g finely ground unrefined sea salt (2%)*
	100 g leaven (20%)

1

SET THE LEAVEN

Measure out 40 g starter (which has been at room temperature for 6–24 hours since the last feeding), 30 g water, 15 g strong white bread flour and 15 g fine wholegrain emmer flour. Mix well, cover the bowl and allow the leaven to mature for 2–4 hours. Put the starter back in the refrigerator.

2

MIX FLOUR, WATER AND LEAVEN (AUTOLYSIS)

Pour 375–425 g water into the bowl with the leaven. Dissolve the leaven in the water with your fingers. Add the specified amount of flour. Use your hands to make sure everything is well mixed together. Gather the dough by scraping down the excess from the edges with a spatula. Cover the bowl and let it sit for an hour (set the timer). Then follow the Basic Bread recipe from step 3 (see page 50).

SPROUTED RYE

W hole rye is very conducive to germination. The germinated grains provide a delightful chewy resistance with a strong, sweet flavour. For those who are interested, you can find all the health benefits of sprouted grains online, but we enjoy this grain because of the taste and texture. This is a generic recipe that you can use with any whole grain, but rye germinates more easily than other cereals because it is so robust that the germ usually remains intact.

INGREDIENTS
Baking percentage in parentheses

For the leaven:
40 g mature starter
30 g water at 30°C
15 g strong white bread flour
15 g fine wholegrain spelt flour

For the bread dough:
100 g whole rye for germination (20%)
150 g fine wholegrain spelt flour (30%)
350 g of strong white bread flour (70%)
350–375 g water at 30°C (70–75%)
10 g finely ground unrefined sea salt (2%)
100 g leaven (20%)

ADDITIONAL EQUIPMENT

2–4-litre mixing bowl, sieve and linen cloth.

1

SPROUT THE WHOLE GRAINS, 2–3 DAYS BEFORE BAKING

A variety of tools for germinating grains are available, but you can also improvise with an ordinary sieve. Put 100 g whole rye in the sieve and rinse well under running cold water. Line a 2–4-litre mixing bowl with a linen cloth or clean kitchen towel, then place the sieve in the bowl over the cloth. Be sure to leave enough of the cloth outside the bowl to drape it over the sieve again. Fill a jug with cold water and pour it over the grains. Fold the cloth over the sieve and pour in more water so that the cloth is also wet. If the grains dry out, the germination will not start. The watering can be repeated up to four times a day, but one watering every morning and evening is generally sufficient, depending on how warm your kitchen is. The warmer it is, the faster the grains will germinate; however, the warmer it is, the faster the grains will dry out between watering. You can tell that the grain is germinating as soon as a seedling appears. This usually takes 2 to 3 days, but it can be faster. You will eventually get longer sprouts and as soon as these appear, the grain is ready. Do not let them grow too far because the grains will become plants and lose a lot of flavour.

2

SET THE LEAVEN

Measure out 40 g starter (which has been at room temperature for 6–24 hours since the last feeding), 30 g water, 15 g strong white bread flour and 15 g fine wholegrain spelt flour. Mix well, cover the bowl and allow the leaven to mature for 2–4 hours. Put the starter back in the refrigerator.

3

MIX FLOUR, WATER AND LEAVEN (AUTOLYSIS)

Pour 350–375 g water into the bowl with the leaven. Dissolve the leaven in the water with your fingers. Add the flours and use your hands to make sure everything is well mixed. Gather the dough by scraping down the excess from the edges with a spatula. Cover the bowl and let it sit for an hour (set the timer). Then add the sprouted grains when you add the salt, following step 3 of the Basic Bread recipe (see page 50), and follow the rest of the steps accordingly.

PAIN DE CAMPAGNE

O riginally, pain de campagne was intended to feed an entire family for several days. In the French countryside, there were municipal ovens to which each household would bring their dough and bake it together with their neighbour's bread. At the time, bread was usually coarser than it is today as there were no industrial grain mills. It was also common to include a small proportion of rye in your bread – it is said that the rye was automatically included as it grew as a 'weed' in the wheat fields, and therefore inevitably formed part of the milled flour.

Nowadays, there are an incredible number of variations of country bread, but what is common with most of them is that it is relatively light in colour, with an airy, moist and light crumb. Chad Robertson of Tartine Bakery in San Francisco has set the standard with his basic country loaf – a bread that has revolutionised home baking in many countries. Of all the bakers we have been influenced by and learned from, Robertson and his original approach has undoubtedly inspired us the most.

Our country bread is baked with 5% fine wholegrain rye, in addition to the wholegrain rye in the leaven. This rye contributes to an active fermentation and gives sweetness and character to the dough. This is a mild bread, which is delicious to break off and eat as is, or serve with other food.

INGREDIENTS
Baking percentage in parentheses

For the leaven:	For the bread dough:
40 g mature starter	*400 g strong white bread flour (80%)*
30 g water at 30°C	*75 g fine wholegrain wheat flour (15%)*
15 g strong white bread flour	*25 g fine wholegrain rye flour (5%)*
15 g fine wholegrain rye flour	*350–425 g water at 30°C (75–85%)*
	10 g finely ground unrefined sea salt (2%)
	100 g leaven (20%)

1

SET THE LEAVEN

Measure out 40 g starter (which has been at room temperature for
6–24 hours since the last feeding), 30 g water, 15 g strong white bread flour and 15 g fine
wholegrain rye flour. Mix well, cover the bowl and allow the leaven to mature for
2–4 hours. Put the starter back in the refrigerator.

2

MIX FLOUR, WATER AND LEAVEN (AUTOLYSIS)

Pour 375–425 g water into the bowl with the leaven. Dissolve the leaven in the water
with your fingers. Add the specified amount of flour. Use your hands to make sure
everything is well mixed together. Gather the dough by scraping down the excess from
the edges with a spatula. Cover the bowl and let it sit for an hour (set the timer).
Then follow the Basic Bread recipe from step 3 (see page 50).

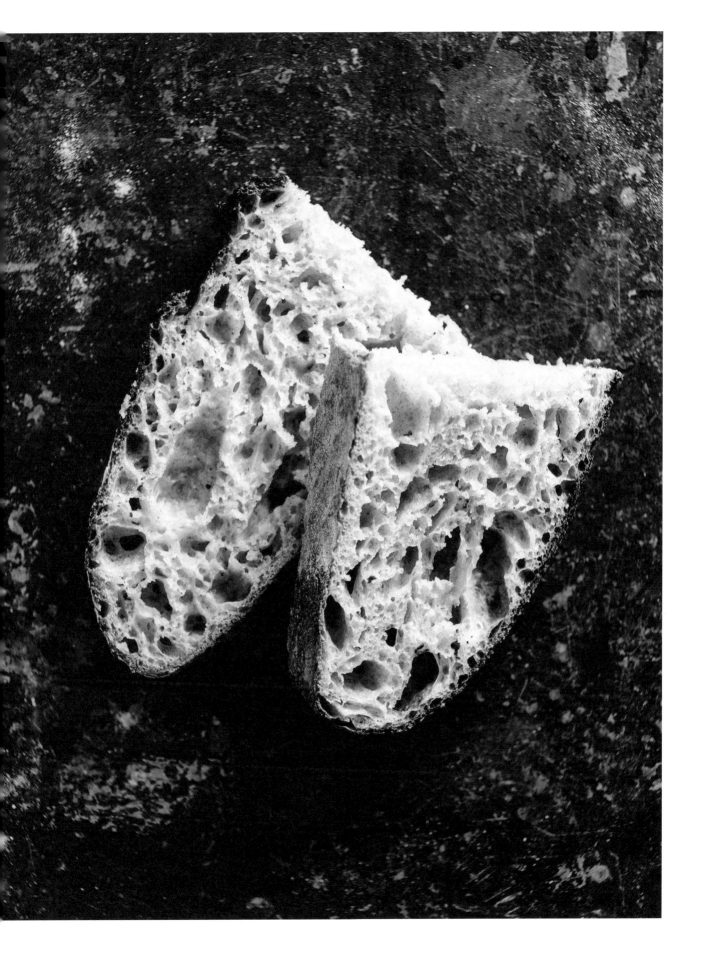

SIFT AND SCALD

T his method involves removing the bran from wholegrain flour and then scalding it in boiling water. The bran swells in the water and absorbs much more water than it would through regular mixing with the dough. This allows you to bake with a higher quantity of water without the dough becoming unmanageable. The act of boiling also brings out a lot of sweetness. This method produces exceptionally moist and sweet-tasting bread, which keeps well for several days. Sifting and scalding works extremely well for wheat, spelt, emmer and einkorn.

INGREDIENTS
Baking percentage in parentheses

For the leaven:
40 g mature starter
30 g water at 30°C
15 g strong white bread flour
15 g fine whole wheat or spelt or emmer flour

For the bread dough:
150 g fine whole wheat or spelt or emmer flour (30%)
350 g strong white bread flour (70%)
425–450 g water at 30°C (75 g of the water is used to boil the bran) (85–90%)
10 g finely ground unrefined sea salt (2%)
100 g leaven (20%)

ADDITIONAL EQUIPMENT

Fine-mesh sieve, a large bowl and a small bowl.

SIFT AND SCALD

Place a fine-mesh sieve over a 2–4-litre bowl. Place the bowl on the scale and measure out 150 g fine whole wheat/spelt/emmer flour into the sieve. Sift out the bran and pour it into a smaller bowl. You will end up with about 20–30 g bran. Steep the bran in 75 g boiling water and let it sit for 4–10 hours.

SET THE LEAVEN

Measure out 40 g starter (which has been at room temperature for 6–24 hours since the last feeding), 30 g water, 15 g strong white bread flour and 15 g fine whole wheat flour. Mix well, cover the bowl and allow the leaven to mature over 2–4 hours. Put the starter back in the refrigerator.

3

MIX FLOUR, WATER AND LEAVEN (AUTOLYSIS)

Pour 350 g water into the bowl with the leaven. Dissolve the leaven in the water with your fingers. Add the specified amount of flour, including what you sifted (the bran is not yet included). Use your hands to make sure everything is well mixed together. Gather the dough by scraping down the excess from the edges with a spatula. Cover the bowl and let the dough sit for an hour (set the timer). Add the boiled bran when adding the salt in step 3 of the Basic Bread recipe (see page 50) and follow the rest of the steps accordingly.

KHORASAN WHEAT

B read with a lot of khorasan wheat (which is the origin of common durum wheat) has a golden amber tone and a moist and porous crumb. The flavour is sweet and corn-like, especially the crust, which becomes extra crunchy. khorasan wheat, also known commercially as Kamut, is a so-called hard wheat with a very high protein content. This means you have to use quite a lot of water in the dough to make the bread moist. khorasan wheat has quite good baking properties, so we can easily increase the amount of whole grain used to 50% without sacrificing volume and crumb.

INGREDIENTS
Baking percentage in parentheses

For the leaven:	For the bread dough:
40 g mature starter	*250 g fine wholegrain khorasan wheat flour (50%)*
30 g water at 30°C	*250 g strong white bread flour (50%)*
15 g strong white bread flour	*425–450 g water at 30°C (80–90%)*
15 g fine wholegrain khorasan wheat flour	*10 g finely ground unrefined sea salt (2%)*
	100 g leaven (20%)

1

SET THE LEAVEN

Measure out 40 g starter (which has been at room temperature for 6–24 hours since the last feeding), 30 g water, 15 g strong white bread flour and 15 g fine wholegrain khorasan wheat flour. Mix well, cover the bowl and allow the leaven to mature over 2–4 hours. Put the starter back in the refrigerator.

MIX FLOUR, WATER AND LEAVEN (AUTOLYSIS)

Pour 375–425 g water into the bowl with the leaven. Dissolve the leaven in the water with your fingers. Add the specified amount of flour. Use your hands to make sure everything is well mixed together. Gather the dough by scraping down the excess from the edges with a spatula. Cover the bowl and let it sit for an hour (set the timer). Then follow the Basic Bread recipe from step 3 (see page 50).

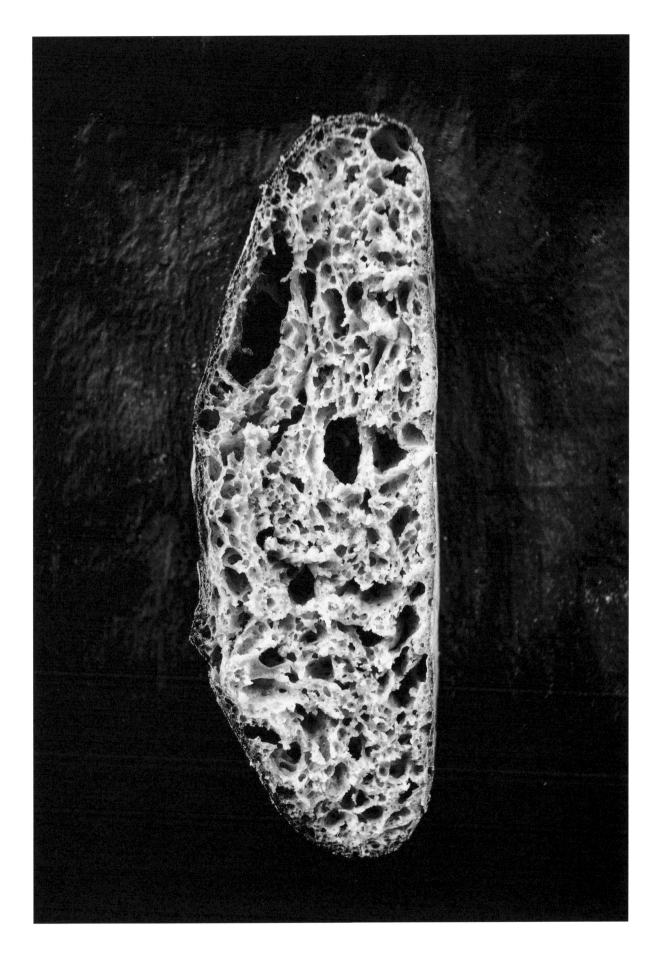

TIN LOAF

We wanted to add a classic tin loaf recipe among all the hearth loaves, not only because we love this bread style, but also to add an alternative for those who don't have the space or equipment to make hearth loaves. The method is exactly the same as for the other loaves, but instead of placing the loaf in a proving basket after shaping, you put it in 1 kg loaf tin.

We prefer to oil the tin with rapeseed oil (which, in our opinion, is an excellent complement to the bread).

We don't score this loaf, and instead aim for a deeply golden, blistered crust. This also makes the risk of over-proving less precarious, as the dough doesn't lose any volume by puncturing the surface.

This loaf is perfect to freeze in slices and defrost in the toaster. It's also very practical for families, as you're able to bake several loaves in the oven at the same time. We usually take the loaf out of the tin after 30 minutes, place it on its side, and turn the heat up to give it a rustic and crackling crust. Turn it over after about 5 minutes.

INGREDIENTS
Baking percentage in parentheses

For the leaven:	For the bread dough:
40 g mature starter	100 g fine wholegrain wheat flour (20%)
30 g water at 30°C	400 g strong white bread flour (80%)
15 g fine wholegrain wheat flour	375–425 g of water at 30°C (75–85%)
15 g strong white bread flour	10 g finely ground unrefined sea salt (2%)
	100 g leaven

1

SET THE LEAVEN

Measure out 40 g starter (which has been at room temperature for 6–24 hours
since the last feeding), 30 g water, 15 g fine wholegrain wheat flour and 15 g strong white
bread flour. Mix well, cover the bowl and allow the leaven to mature for 2–4 hours.
Put the starter back in the refrigerator.

2

MIX FLOUR, WATER AND LEAVEN (AUTOLYSIS)

Pour 375–425 g water into the bowl with the leaven. Dissolve the leaven in the
water with your fingers. Add the specified amount of flour. Use your hands to
make sure everything is well mixed together. Gather the dough by scraping down
the excess from the edges with a spatula. Cover the bowl and let it sit for an hour
(set the timer). Then follow the Basic Bread recipe from step 3 (see page 50),
but leave the dough to prove in the loaf tin instead of the proving basket.

EINKORN

E inkorn has a stronger flavour than most other wheat varieties and is rich in beta-carotene (the orange pigment also found in carrots), which gives the dough a light amber tone. Bread made with a lot of einkorn also produces a thick and extra crispy crust.

Einkorn is among the oldest of the known grains. Along with emmer, it is one of the ancestors of the wheat family, which includes spelt and descendants of country wheat varieties. It also has the highest protein content of all wheat types, but it doesn't have better baking properties than conventional wheat since the protein quality is generally worse. The protein quality has to do with the protein's ability to form gluten bonds. Einkorn also has poor starch gelatinisation, which makes the dough feel sticky. For these reasons, it is perhaps the most difficult grain to bake with in the whole wheat family. Therefore, we only use 30% wholegrain einkorn in this recipe. As with all ancient grains, however, the kind of environment in which the grain is grown leads to substantial variations. If you are able to find einkorn that has been grown under ideal conditions, it will make it that much easier to bake with and you will be able to increase the proportion of einkorn in the dough.

INGREDIENTS

Baking percentage in parentheses

For the leaven:	For the bread dough:
40 g mature starter	*150 g fine wholegrain einkorn flour (30%)*
30 g water at 30°C	*350 g strong white bread flour (70%)*
15 g strong white bread flour	*400-450 g water at 30°C (80-90%)*
15 g fine wholegrain einkorn flour	*10 g finely ground unrefined sea salt (2%)*
	100 g leaven (20%)

SET THE LEAVEN

Measure out 40 g mature starter (which has been at room temperature for 6–24 hours since the last feeding), 30 g water, 15 g strong white bread flour and 15 g fine wholegrain einkorn flour. Mix well, cover the bowl and allow the leaven to mature for 2–4 hours. Put the starter back in the refrigerator.

MIX FLOUR, WATER AND LEAVEN (AUTOLYSIS)

Pour 375–425 g water into the bowl with the leaven. Dissolve the leaven in the water with your fingers. Add the specified amount of flour. Use your hands to make sure everything is well mixed together. Gather the dough by scraping down the excess from the edges with a spatula. Cover the bowl and let it sit for an hour (set the timer). Then follow the Basic Bread recipe from step 3 (see page 50).

100% SPELT

W ith regard to taste, there is little that can compare with this bread and by baking it you really get to know the characteristics of the spelt grain. A dark and rich crumb comes together with a thick and crispy crust with intense flavours from the caramelisation. Be sure to observe the fermentation process, as wholegrain flour ferments faster than sifted flour, because of higher enzyme activity, so it can definitely get away from you. This recipe contains only wholegrain flour, with the exception of the leaven. Fresh wholegrain flour ground on stone has a slightly sticky consistency precisely because the oils are preserved. Beneficial nutrients are also preserved because very little heat is generated by the slow-moving rocks when the grain is ground.

INGREDIENTS

Baking percentage in parentheses

For the leaven:
40 g mature starter
30 g water at 30°C
15 g strong white bread flour
15 g fine wholegrain spelt flour

For the bread dough:
500 g fine wholegrain spelt flour (100%)
400–450 g water at 30°C (80–90%)
10 g finely ground unrefined sea salt (2%)
100 g leaven (20%)

1

SET THE LEAVEN

Measure out 40 g mature starter (which has been at room temperature for 6–24 hours since the last feeding), 30 g water, 15 g strong white bread flour and 15 g fine wholegrain spelt flour. Mix well, cover the bowl and allow the leaven to mature for 2–4 hours. Put the starter back in the refrigerator.

2

MIX FLOUR, WATER AND LEAVEN (AUTOLYSIS)

Pour 400–450 g water into the bowl with the leaven. Dissolve the leaven in the water with your fingers. Add the specified amount of flour. Use your hands to make sure everything is well mixed together. Gather the dough by scraping down the excess from the edges with a spatula. Cover the bowl and let it sit for an hour (set the timer). Then follow the Basic Bread recipe from step 3 (see page 50).

WHOLE NAKED BARLEY

N aked barley is one of the oldest grains we have. It is called 'naked' because the outer shell falls off during threshing, while ordinary barley must be shelled and polished during processing. Naked barley has a smooth and mild taste. When working with grains that do not have particularly good baking properties, we use it to provide taste and character rather than as part of the chemistry of the dough. There are several ways to do this and one of the best methods is to boil the grain and then add it after the dough has formed its gluten bonds. The boiling brings out a lot of its natural sweetness and the soft grain kernel produces a moist texture in the crumb.

You can replace the naked barley with other whole grains, such as ordinary barley. You can also ferment the whole grains after they have been boiled. Adding a teaspoon of starter to the boiled grains and allowing this to sit for 6–10 hours will add fresh acidity and give a whole new character to the bread. Experiment!

INGREDIENTS

Baking percentage in parentheses

For the leaven:
40 g mature starter
30 g water 30°C
15 g strong white bread flour
15 g fine wholegrain spelt flour

For the bread dough:
100 g whole naked barley or barley (20%)
200 g water for soaking the grain (20%)
150 g fine wholegrain spelt flour (30%)
350 g strong white bread flour (70%)
350–375 g water 30°C (70–75%)
10 g finely ground unrefined sea salt (2%)
100 g leaven (20%)

1

24 HOURS BEFORE SETTING THE LEAVEN

Soak 100 g whole naked barley in 100 g cold water.
Allow to sit for 8–12 hours (or overnight).

12 HOURS BEFORE SETTING THE LEAVEN

Add 100 g scalding water to the same bowl.
Allow to sit for 4–12 hours.

2

SET THE LEAVEN

Measure out 40 g mature starter (which has been at room temperature for 6–24 hours since the last feeding), 30 g water, 15 g strong white bread and 15 g fine wholegrain spelt flour. Mix well, cover the bowl and allow the leaven to mature for 2–4 hours.
Put the starter back in the refrigerator.

3

MIX FLOUR, WATER AND LEAVEN (AUTOLYSIS)

Pour 350 –375 g water into the bowl with leaven. Dissolve the leaven in the water with your fingers. Add the specified amount of flour. Use your hands to make sure everything is well mixed together. Gather the dough by scraping down the excess from the edges with a spatula. Cover the bowl and let it sit for an hour (set the timer). Add the boiled grains when adding the salt in step 3 of the Basic Bread recipe (see page 50) and follow the rest of the recipe accordingly.

TOASTED OATS

M ost people have some kind of relationship with oats as few grains have so much character and taste. Like barley, however, oat flour has poor baking properties, so we use oats as an addition to add flavour. We toast them in flake form in the oven before we soak them. Toasting gives a wonderfully earthy and full-bodied character to the bread. You can of course use grains or flakes of other varieties too, but be aware that some grains, such as rye and barley, are harder and take longer to become soft when soaked. When using harder grains, boil the flakes in double the amount of boiling water. We like to coat this bread in oat flakes. Sprinkle the oats on a plate and roll the dough over the flakes before putting it in the proving basket. When doing this, we recommend that you cut the bread with scissors rather than score it.

INGREDIENTS
Baking percentage in parentheses

For the leaven:
40 g mature starter
30 g water at 30°C
15 g strong white bread flour
15 g fine wholegrain spelt flour

For the bread dough:
100 g oats (20%)
100 g water for soaking the oats (20%)
150 g fine wholegrain spelt flour (30%)
350 g strong white bread flour (70%)
350–375 g water at 30°C (70–75%)
10 g finely ground unrefined sea salt (2%)
100 g leaven (20%)

1

TOAST AND SOAK THE OATS

This is perfect to do at the same time as feeding your starter in the morning. Preheat the oven to 170°C. Measure out 100 g oats and spread them over a clean baking sheet or in a large baking dish; the flakes should not overlap. Toast in the oven for 10 minutes. Allow to cool for a few minutes before putting the oats in a bowl and adding 100 g room temperature water. Cover and let sit for 4–10 hours.

2

SET THE LEAVEN

Measure out 40 g mature starter (which has been at room temperature for 6–24 hours since the last feeding), 30 g water, 15 g strong white bread flour and 15 g fine wholegrain spelt flour. Mix well, cover the bowl and allow the leaven to mature for 2–4 hours. Put the starter back in the refrigerator.

3

MIX FLOUR, WATER AND LEAVEN (AUTOLYSIS)

Pour 350–375 g water into the bowl with the leaven. Dissolve the leaven in the water with your fingers. Add the specified amount of flour. Use your hands to make sure everything is well mixed together. Gather the dough by scraping down the excess from the edges with a spatula. Cover on the bowl and let it sit for an hour (set the timer). Add the toasted and soaked flakes when adding the salt in step 3 of the Basic Bread recipe (see page 50) and follow the rest of the steps accordingly.

FRIENDSHIP BREAD

arly on, we discovered a diverse baking environment on Instagram, where we could see and be inspired by what others were doing around the world. For home-bakers like us, this was a rewarding place to exchange recipes and experiments.

Jonas Rieback (@jonas_rieback) and Martin Westin (@leveriktigtbrod) from Sweden are the two with whom we've had the most contact. Both bake wonderful sourdough bread and have the same passion for fine ingredients as we do. They also claim that the best bread is often baked at home. After exchanging lots of ideas, we ended up with a rustic loaf with toasted flakes of naked barley or ordinary barley boiled in beer. You can use whatever kind of beer you want, but we believe a good choice is a hoppy beer such as an IPA. A strong aroma of hops comes through as well as the sweet, full flavour of whole barley flakes.

INGREDIENTS
Baking percentage in parentheses

For the leaven:
40 g mature starter
30 g water at 30°C
15 g strong white bread flour
15 g fine wholegrain spelt flour

For the bread dough:
100 g barley flakes (20%)
200 g light beer (40%)
500 g strong white bread flour (100%)
350-375 g water at 30°C (70-75%)
10 g finely ground unrefined sea salt (2%)
100 g leaven (20%)

1

TOAST BARLEY FLAKES AND BOIL IN BEER

Preheat the oven to 170°C. Give the beer a quick boil and set aside. Spread out the barley flakes in a roasting tin and toast them in the oven for 10 minutes. Let them cool slightly before you pour them into a bowl and add the beer. Cover and let sit for 4–8 hours.

2

SET THE LEAVEN

Measure out 40 g mature starter (which has been at room temperature for 6–24 hours since the last feeding), 30 g water, 15 g strong white bread flour and 15 g fine wholegrain spelt flour. Mix well, cover the bowl and allow the leaven to mature over 2–4 hours. Put the starter back in the refrigerator.

3

MIX FLOUR, WATER AND LEAVEN (AUTOLYSIS)

Pour 350–375 g water into the bowl with the leaven. Dissolve the leaven in the water with your fingers. Add the specified amount of flour. Use your hands to make sure everything is well mixed together. Gather the dough by scraping down the excess from the edges with a spatula. Cover the bowl and let it sit for an hour (set the timer). Add in the toasted and soaked flakes when adding the salt in step 3 of the Basic Bread recipe (see page 50) and follow the rest of the steps accordingly.

6

RESOURCES

INGREDIENT SUPPLIERS

A wide range of organic flours can be found in local supermarkets, but for specialist grains and the best ingredients, finding your local artisan producer is undoubtedly the best course of action. Nonetheless, if you're not lucky enough to be in an area near a small mill or farm, then the following suppliers might prove useful as many take online orders or can direct you to their stockists.

BACHELDRE WATERMILL – An organic mill, producing a range of flour blends, which can be purchased through their website or in store from Waitrose or John Lewis. www.bacheldremill.co.uk

CALBOURNE WATER MILL – This mill on the Isle of Wight hosts events and courses. Their flours can be bought online and at local shops. www.calbournewatermill.co.uk

CRAKEHALL WATERMILL – Working watermill and guesthouse based in North Yorkshire, using authentic 19th-century equipment. Their flours are sold in a range of local bakeries and shops in Yorkshire, and are available through their website. www.crakehallwatermill.co.uk

COGGLESFORD MILL – A beautiful watermill that is open to the public. Stoneground organic wholemeal flour can be bought on site. www.cogglesfordmillsleaford.co.uk

DOVES FARM – Established in 1978, Doves Farm is a respected specialist in organic flours. Their flour blends can be purchased through many stores nationwide or online. www.dovesfarm.co.uk

FOSTERS MILL, SWAFFHAM PRIOR – This windmill produces flour from locally-grown, organic wheat. Their flour can be ordered online or bought from local shops. www.priorsflour.co.uk

FELIN GANOL WATERMILL – Producers of quality, organic stoneground flours that can be bought from the mill or local stockists. www. felinganol.co.uk

GILCHESTERS ORGANICS – Gilchesters grow heritage wheat varieties using organic methods. Their stoneground flour, which is milled on site, can be bought from a number of stockists in northern England and Scotland. www.gilchesters.com

HEATHERSLAW CORN MILL – As well as being open for public visits, Heatherslaw Corn Mill is a working mill, and sells its own flour blends at the mill and online. www.ford-and-etal.co.uk/heatherslaw-mill

HOLLAND & BARRETT – Stocking a wide range of grains in store and online, including spelt, rye and amaranth flour. Over 620 stores around the UK and Ireland. www.hollandandbarrett.com

LITTLE SALKELD WATERMILL – Based in Cumbria, Little Salkeld Watermill runs regular bread-making courses, as well as selling its own flour and other products. www.organicmill.co.uk

MARRIAGE'S MILL – Marriage's offer a wide range of bread making, culinary, organic and speciality flours, including stoneground wholemeal flour traditionally milled on horizontal French Burr stones. www.marriagesmillers.co.uk

MATTHEWS COTSWOLD FLOUR – Used by cooks, chefs and artisan home bakers all over the country, Matthews produce a range of organic flours, including spelt and rye. www.fwpmatthews.co.uk

MUNGOSWELL MALT & MILLING – Scottish mill based in East Lothian, selling a range of organic and non-organic flour online, suitable for artisan bread and cake baking. www.mungoswells.co.uk

PLANET ORGANIC – A growing number of stores and a useful online retailer stocking a range of organic heritage grains and flours. Also offers Doves Farm produce (see left). www.planetorganic.com

SHARPHAM PARK – A family-run mill, specialising in organic stoneground spelt flour, sold through their website. www.sharphampark.com

SHIPTON MILL – Key suppliers for home bakers and restaurants alike, their blends can be purchased through their website, as well as in wholefood shops and markets around the country. www.shipton-mill.com

STOATE & SONS – Established in 1832, Stoate & Sons are flour millers based in Dorset. Their flours are sold in a range of bakeries and health food shops around South West England, as well as on their website. www.stoatesflour.co.uk

STOTFOLD WATERMILL – Based in Bedfordshire, this independent watermill is open to the public, and also produces a range of wholemeal and white flours. www.stotfoldmill.com

WALK MILL – Based in Cheshire and specialising in stoneground flour; the mill is open daily, and their flours are sold in a number of local shops and bakeries. www.walkmillflour.co.uk

WESSEX MILL – With over hundred years' milling history, Wessex Mill produces and sells bread flour, and specialist grains, as well as sourdough starters. www.wessexmill.co.uk

WRIGHT'S BAKING – A family-run business producing a range of bread flours, grain mixes especially designed for homebakers. www.wrightsflour.co.uk

EQUIPMENT SUPPLIERS

O n pages 42–3 you will find the key pieces of equipment required to make the recipes in this book. Most of these items are widely available and easy to find, but the following stockists will be able help you out with some of the more unusual items.

BAKERY BITS – Online artisan baking specialists, based in Somerset and selling a range of artisan baking equipment, from bread peels to baking stones, from proving baskets to bannetons, as well as sourdough starters and a range of organic flours. www.bakerybits.co.uk

HOBBS HOUSE BAKERY – Everything from complete bread making kits that include multi-award winning 61 year old sourdough starter to dough scrapers. All used and tested to meet the demanding standards exacted by a 90 year old artisan bakery. www.hobbshousebakery.co.uk

JOHN LEWIS – A leading department store in the UK, with an extensive range of artisan baking equipment online and in stores around the UK. www.johnlewis.com

LAKELAND – A specialist in cookware, selling a range of baking utensils and artisan baking equipment, including cast iron pots, proving baskets (bannetons) and a range of mixing bowls. These can be purchased online or in over 70 stores nationwide. www.lakeland.co.uk

LE CREUSET – A leading producer of cookware since the 1920s, Le Creuset produce a range of dishes, tins and cast iron pots. These can be purchased online, in Le Creuset specific stores or in a wide range of independent cookshops and larger UK chains, including John Lewis and House of Fraser. www.lecreuset.co.uk

NISBETS – Baking equipment suppliers for both businesses and keen home bakers, based in Bristol. www.nisbets.co.uk

SOUS CHEF – Online ingredient and equipment specialist for adventurous cooks and artisan bakers. www.souschef.co.uk

SCHOOLS AND SOCIETIES

I t will come as no surprise to find there is a vibrant community of sourdough bakers in the world and a host of friendly and supportive websites and schools .

THE BERTINET KITCHEN – Based in Bath and run by French chef and baker Richard Bertinet, this cookery school runs a range of bakery and bread-making courses, suitable for amateur bakers and professionals alike. www.thebertinetkitchen.com

THE FRESH LOAF – International community site for amateur artisan bakers. Includes a wealth of information including forums and more. www.thefreshloaf.com

REAL BREAD CAMPAIGN – International online network to support and promote baking without the use of processing aids or additional additives. As well as online support the campaign holds regular community run events throughout the UK. www.realbreadcampaign.org

RIOT RYE BAKEHOUSE – Award-winning baker Joe Fitzmaurice runs a host of hands-on courses at the Riot Rye Bakehouse in Tipperary. www.riotrye.ie

SCHOOL OF ARTISAN FOOD – Based in the heart of the Sherwood Forest, the school runs a variety of short courses, including baking and artisan bread-making for a range of experience levels. www.schoolofartisanfood.org

SOURDOUGH LIBRARY – Online international index and reference site for amateur bakers, listing articles, recipes, tutorial videos, blogs, forums and other information relating to sourdough and artisan baking. www.sourdoughlibrary.org

THE SOURDOUGH SCHOOL – An expert tuition school run by Vanessa Kimbell in Northamptonshire; as well as running courses, the Sourdough School has advice and further recipes on their website and excellent links to artisan suppliers and mills. www.sourdough.co.uk

SOURDOUGH NATION – A fun and active forum run by Hobbs House Bakery, with over 4,000 members and a range of discussion boards on sourdough and artisan baking, for sharing advice and recipes. Sourdough courses for all levels are taught in the bakery school. www.hobbshousebakery.co.uk/forum/ sourdoughnation

TRACEBRIDGE SOURDOUGH – Run by Gordon Woodcock and Katie Venner, self-taught sourdough enthusiasts, from a shed and a brick oven in the woods outside Wellington, Somerset. Offers classes in baking as well as other food and drinks. www.tracebridgesourdough.co.uk

First published in Great Britain in 2017 by Modern Books
An imprint of Elwin Street Productions Limited
14 Clerkenwell Green
London EC1R 0DP
United Kingdom
Tel: +44 (0) 207 253 3044
www.modern-books.com

Published originally under the title *Surdeig* by Casper André Lugg and Martin
Ivar Hveem Fjeld. First published by Forlaget Vigmostad & Bjørke, Norway, in
2015. Published by agreement with the Kontext Agency.

Design: Simen Grytøyr
Contributing editor: Drew Smith
Translator: Tynlee Roberts

Picture credits:
Miłosz Guzowski/Alamy Stock Photo, 14-15;
ImageBROKER/Alamy Stock Photo, 32.
All other photography by Simen Grytøyr

ISBN 978-1-911130-05-5
10 9 8 7 6

Printed in China